FROM CHALKBOARD TO CYBER THREATS: GUIDING SCHOOLS TO DIGITAL SAFETY

DR DHEERAJ MEHROTRA

Made with ♥ on the Notion Press Platform
www.notionpress.com

Contents

Preface

Education has always evolved—from oral traditions to chalkboards, from textbooks to smart classrooms. Today, as schools embrace digital tools and online platforms, they also face a new and complex reality: the growing landscape of cyber risks. From Chalkboard to Cyber Threats: Guiding Schools to Digital Safety is written in response to this urgent shift, where technology has become both a powerful enabler of learning and a potential source of vulnerability.

This book is not meant to create fear, but awareness. Schools are no longer confined within physical walls; they operate in a digital ecosystem that includes learning management systems, student data, online assessments, communication platforms, and social media. With this expansion comes the responsibility to protect students, educators, and institutions from cyber threats, data breaches, misinformation, and unsafe digital practices.

The purpose of this book is to simplify digital safety for school leaders, teachers, parents, and policymakers. It bridges the gap between technology and education by explaining cyber risks in clear, practical language and offering actionable strategies that schools can realistically implement. From understanding basic cyber hygiene and data privacy to building a culture of digital responsibility and resilience, the focus remains firmly on prevention, preparedness, and ethical use of technology.

Most importantly, this book reinforces a critical message: digital safety is not solely a technical issue—it is an educational and leadership responsibility. Just as schools teach discipline, values, and citizenship in the physical world, they must now do so in the digital world.

As schools continue their journey from chalkboards to connected classrooms, this book aims to serve as a trusted guide—helping institutions safeguard learning, protect young minds, and confidently navigate the challenges of the digital age.

Dr Dheeraj Mehrotra

CHAPTER ONE

From Chalkboard to Cyber Threats

DIGITAL SAFETY IN EDUCATION

From Chalkboard to Cyber Threats: Guiding Schools To Digital Safety

Navigating the intersection of digital transformation and cybersecurity in India's educational landscape

Dr Dheeraj Mehrotra

Cyber safety is not optional; it is essential in a digital world.

Chapter 1

The Digital Transformation of Indian Schools

A smart click today can prevent a cyber crisis tomorrow.

Chalkboards to Laptops: A Revolution in Education

Digital India Initiative

India's rapid adoption of digital tools in classrooms accelerated significantly post-2015 with the ambitious Digital India initiative, bringing technology to millions of students.

NEP 2020 Impact

The National Education Policy 2020 has been a catalyst, accelerating ICT integration across schools nationwide and setting ambitious digital learning targets.

Pandemic Acceleration

COVID-19 drove a massive shift: Over 250 million students transitioned to online learning platforms, fundamentally changing educational delivery models.

Digital freedom works best when protected by digital responsibility.

India's Educational Leap: From Chalkboards to Digital Futures

Witness the remarkable transformation of India's classrooms, evolving from traditional teaching methods to dynamic digital learning environments. This shift redefines how knowledge is shared and acquired across the nation.

Cyber security begins with awareness, not technology alone.

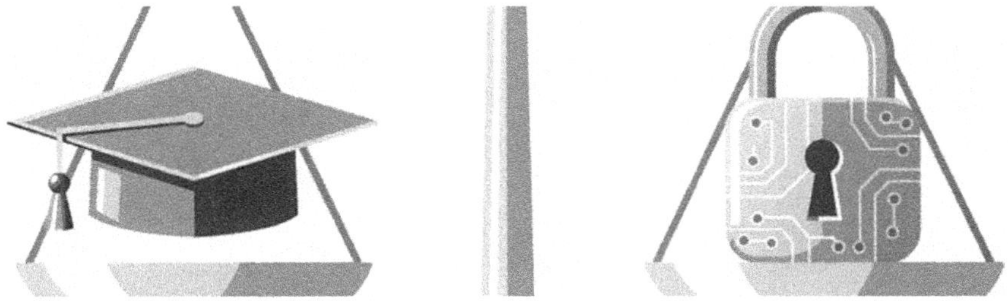

The Promise and Peril of Digital Education

The Promise

- Enhanced access to quality educational resources
- Personalized learning pathways for diverse learners
- Administrative efficiency and streamlined operations
- Collaborative learning beyond physical boundaries

The Peril

- Increased exposure to sophisticated cyber threats
- Data vulnerability and privacy concerns
- Digital addiction and mental health risks
- Cyberbullying and online predation

Protecting data is protecting trust.

The Digital Divide in Indian Schools

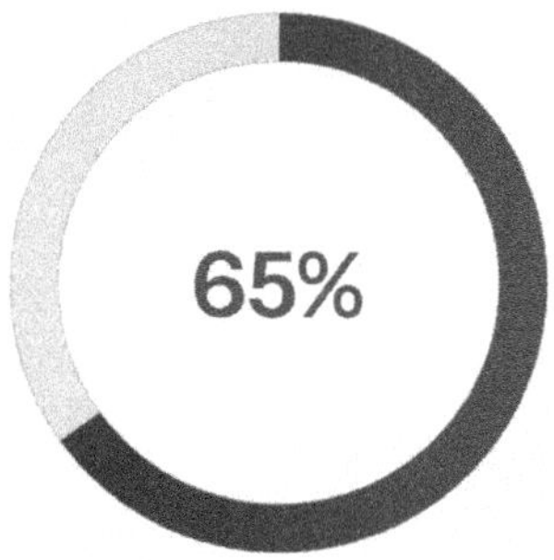

Urban Schools

Have internet connectivity and digital infrastructure

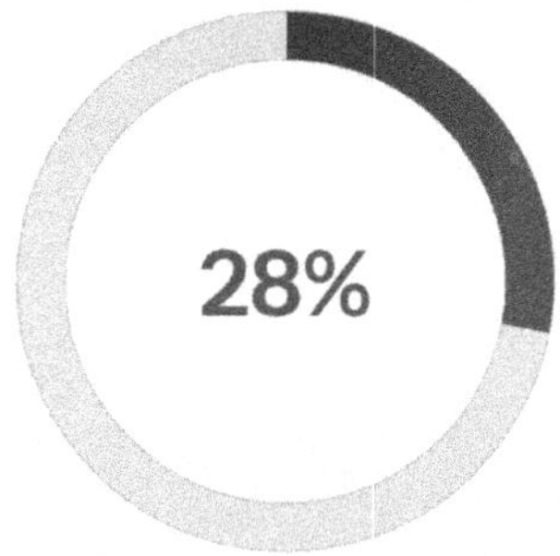

Rural Schools

Have reliable internet access, highlighting stark disparities

Beyond connectivity, schools face challenges with device diversity—ranging from high-end laptops in premium institutions to budget smartphones in rural areas. Digital literacy disparities among teachers and students further complicate the transformation journey.

Every password is a lock—make it strong.

CHAPTER TWO

The Rising Cyber Threat Landscape In Schools

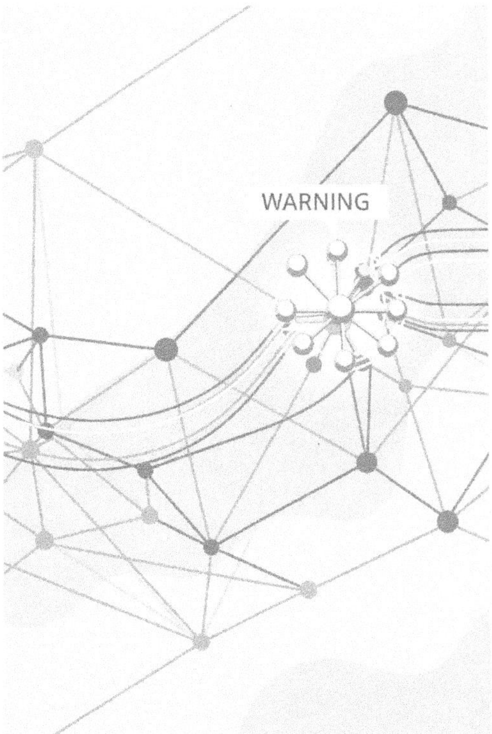

Chapter 2

The Rising Cyber Threat Landscape in Schools

Online safety is a life skill, not a technical skill.

Schools as Prime Cyber Targets

Global Vulnerability

Educational institutions rank among the top 5 sectors targeted by cybercriminals globally, due to valuable data and often inadequate security measures.

Rising Indian Threats

India witnessed a 32% rise in cybercrime against children from 2021 to 2022, according to National Crime Records Bureau (NCRB) data, signalling an alarming trend.

Resource Constraints

Limited cybersecurity budgets and awareness among school administrators increase vulnerability, making schools attractive soft targets for attackers.

Think before you click; not every link is safe.

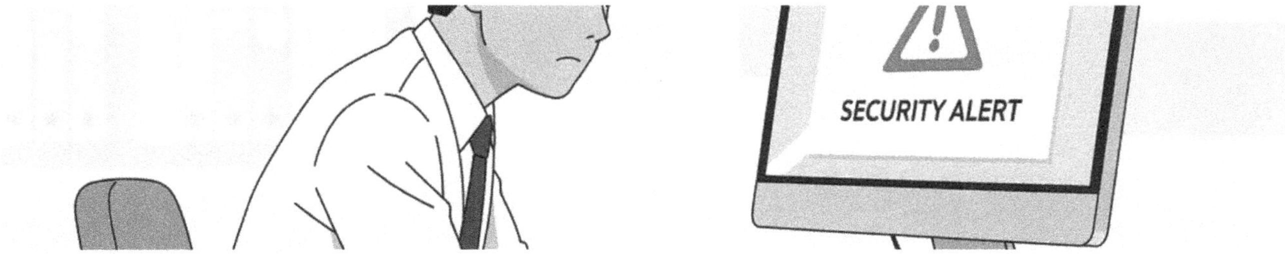

The Cost of Cyberattacks on Schools

Data Breaches

Exposure of student personal information, academic records, grades, and financial data compromises privacy and trust.

Operational Disruptions

System downtime causes significant loss of instructional time, impacting academic calendars and learning outcomes.

Reputational Damage

Security incidents erode stakeholder trust, potentially impacting student enrollment and institutional credibility.

Cyber threats target carelessness more than systems.

The Rising Tide of Cyberattacks in Indian Education

Indian educational institutions face an escalating threat from cyberattacks, ranging from crippling ransomware demands to extensive data breaches. These incidents not only jeopardize sensitive student information and academic continuity but also erode public trust and institutional credibility. Urgent, proactive measures are essential to safeguard the future of digital learning in the region.

Privacy once lost is difficult to regain.

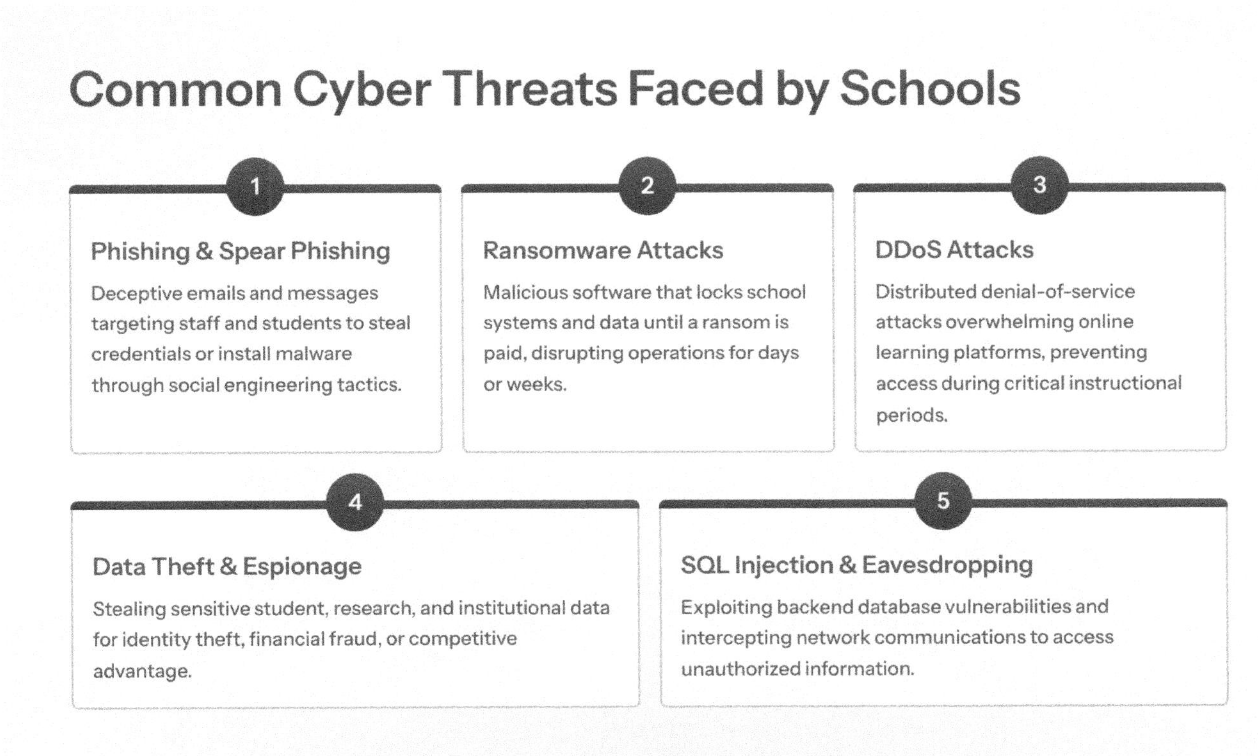

Safe digital habits build secure digital citizens.

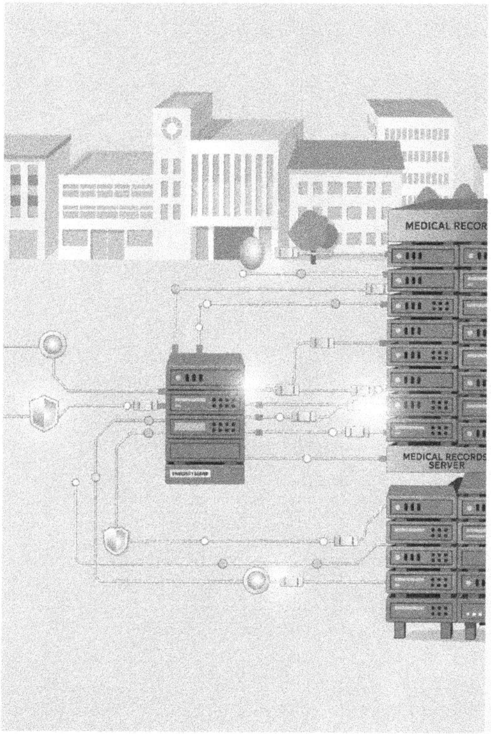

Case Study: University of California, Berkeley Breach

In a sobering example of prolonged security breaches in education, hackers stole 160,000 medical records from UC Berkeley over several months, remaining undetected for an extended period. This case highlights the critical risks of insufficient monitoring and delayed breach detection in the education sector, where sensitive data may be compromised long before discovery.

Cybersecurity is everyone's responsibility, not just IT's job.

CHAPTER THREE

Vulnerabilities Among Students and Educators

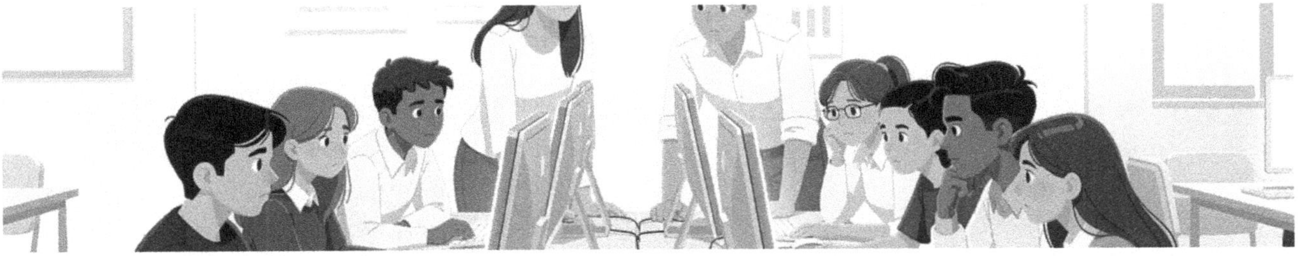

Chapter 3

Vulnerabilities Among Students and Educators

Awareness is the strongest firewall.

Students: The Most Vulnerable Users

Massive Youth Presence

One in three internet users globally is under 18 years old, with children's online presence surging dramatically in recent years.

Multiple Exposures

Young users face cyberbullying, online predators, inappropriate content, and harmful challenges spreading through social platforms.

Low Awareness

Many students lack understanding of privacy risks, safe online behaviour, and the long-term consequences of digital actions.

The internet remembers—post wisely.

Educators' Cybersecurity Awareness Gap

A comprehensive study conducted in Nashik district revealed significant disparities in cybersecurity preparedness. Rural teachers reported substantially less training and institutional support in cyber safety compared to their urban counterparts.

Despite managing sensitive student data daily, many educators remain unaware of fundamental cyber hygiene best practices, including secure password management, recognizing phishing attempts, and protecting confidential information.

Digital convenience must never compromise digital safety.

Digital Addiction and Mental Health Concerns

Increased Screen Time

Pandemic-era surge in device usage continues, with studies linking prolonged screen exposure to stress, anxiety, and sleep disruption among students.

Cyberbullying Impact

Online harassment and exposure to harmful content significantly impact psychological well-being, self-esteem, and academic performance.

Long-term Effects

Persistent digital stressors contribute to depression, social isolation, and difficulty with real-world interpersonal relationships.

A secure system starts with informed users.

The Silent Threat: Cyberbullying

Online harassment casts a long shadow over students' lives, significantly impacting their mental health and academic journey. The relentless exposure to harmful content and digital aggression can erode self-esteem, provoke anxiety, and foster feelings of isolation.

Understanding the profound effects of cyberbullying is essential. It's a critical step toward creating a safer, more supportive digital environment where students can thrive without fear.

Online trust should be earned, not assumed.

CHAPTER FOUR

LEGAL AND POLICY FRAMEWORKS FOR SCHOOL CYBER SAFETY

Chapter 4

Legal and Policy Frameworks for School Cyber Safety

Cyber safety protects identities, futures, and reputations.

National Cyber Safety Guidelines for Schools (NCPCR 2021)

The National Commission for Protection of Child Rights issued comprehensive guidelines emphasizing a holistic approach to digital safety in educational institutions.

01

Cyber Safety Education

Integrating cyber safety awareness and digital literacy across curricula and age groups.

02

Inclusive Access

Ensuring gender-sensitive access to technology and bridging digital divides across socioeconomic groups.

03

Implementation Checklist

Providing schools with actionable protocols for implementing cyber safety measures and incident response.

Data protection is a form of respect.

India's IT Act and Cybercrime Laws

Legal Framework

- Information Technology Act, 2000 (amended 2008)
- Protection of Children from Sexual Offences Act (POCSO), 2012
- Indian Penal Code provisions on cyber offences
- Personal Data Protection Bill (pending)

Key Protections

- Legal recourse for data theft and unauthorized access
- Provisions against cyberbullying and online harassment
- Protection from online exploitation and abuse
- Reporting mechanisms and law enforcement collaboration

Strong passwords are the first line of defence.

Role of National and State Education Boards

Curriculum Integration	Teacher Training	Compliance Monitoring
CBSE, ICSE, and state boards mandating cyber safety modules as part of the core curriculum across grade levels.	Structured programmes training educators and administrators on cyber risk management and digital pedagogy.	Regular assessments ensuring schools meet minimum cybersecurity standards and safety protocols.

Education is the best antivirus.

CHAPTER FIVE

BUILDING CYBER SAFETY AWARENESS IN SCHOOLS

Chapter 5

Building Cyber Safety Awareness in Schools

Technology grows fast; safety awareness must grow faster.

Cyber for YOUth Initiative by DSCI

The Data Security Council of India's flagship programme represents a comprehensive approach to cyber safety education.

Student Education

Interactive modules teaching students about cyber threats, privacy protection, and responsible internet use through age-appropriate content.

Teacher Empowerment

Training educators to create and foster cyber-safe learning environments and serve as digital safety role models.

Student Ambassadors

Empowering students as cyber ambassadors who promote safe practices among peers and younger students.

Cyber security is about prevention, not panic.

Impact of Cyber Safety Training in Indian Schools

10K+

People Trained

Over 10,000 students, parents, and teachers trained across Pune and Tamil Nadu regions through comprehensive programmes.

81%

Knowledge Increase

Significant improvement in cyber safety knowledge post-training, as measured by BRB and Norton partnership assessments.

40+

Schools Reached

More than 40 educational institutions implementing structured cyber safety curricula and protocols.

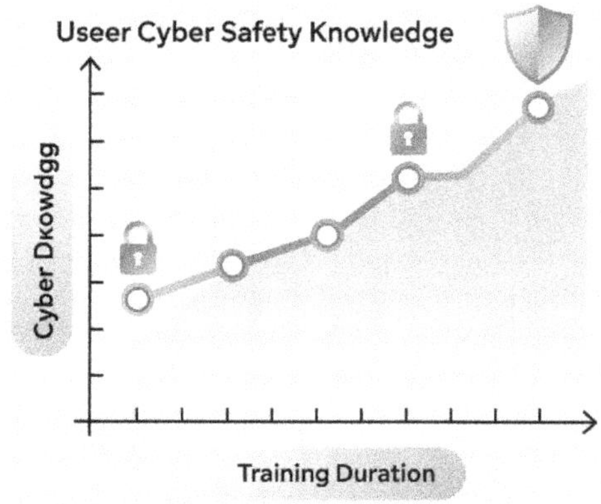

If it sounds too good online, it probably isn't safe.

Community Engagement and Awareness Campaigns

#BeDigiSmart Campaign

A nationwide digital safety movement that has reached over 263,000 people through social media, workshops, and community events.

Key Components:

- Multi-lingual awareness materials for diverse audiences
- Workshops for law enforcement to improve cybercrime reporting and response
- School community events bringing together students, parents, and teachers
- Online resources and helplines for immediate support

Secure behaviour is smarter than secure software alone.

Empowering India's Youth: Cyber Safety in Action

Our interactive workshops are bringing vital cyber safety education directly to students across India. Through engaging sessions and hands-on activities, young participants are not only learning essential digital defense skills but also becoming active advocates for online safety. This enthusiastic engagement is crucial in fostering a generation that is both digitally savvy and secure.

Your digital footprint defines you—walk carefully online.

CHAPTER SIX

Practical Cyber Safety Measures for Schools

Chapter 6

Practical Cyber Safety Measures for Schools

One careless click can undo years of hard work.

Strengthening Infrastructure and Policies

1

Network Security

Implementing secure Wi-Fi networks with robust firewalls, encryption protocols, and network segmentation to isolate sensitive systems.

2

Software Management

Establishing regular software update schedules and systematic patch management to address known vulnerabilities promptly.

3

Access Controls

Deploying multi-factor authentication, role-based access controls, and the principle of least privilege across all school systems.

Cyber safety is modern-day self-defence.

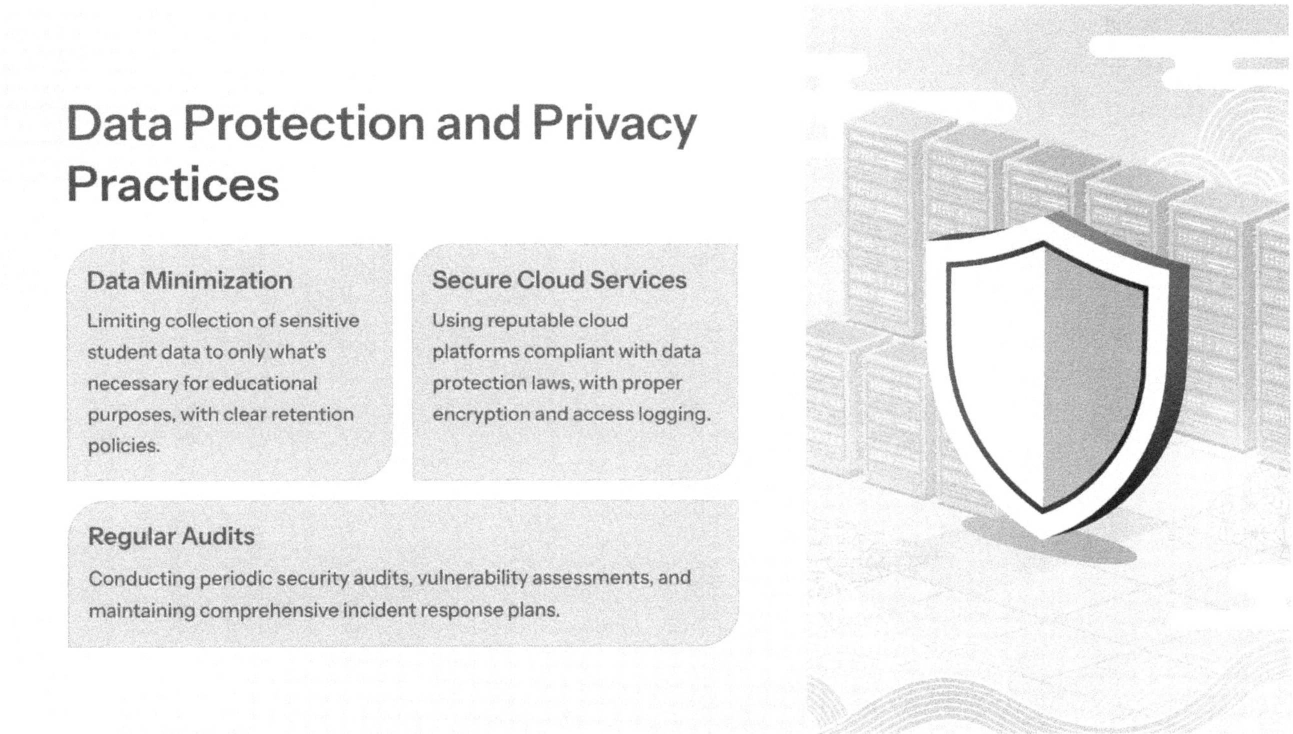

Digital trust depends on digital discipline.

Cyber Hygiene Education for Students and Staff

Strong Password Practices

Creating complex, unique passwords for different accounts and changing them regularly, using password managers when appropriate.

Phishing Recognition

Identifying suspicious emails, links, and attachments; verifying sender identities before clicking or sharing information.

Safe Communication

Practicing responsible social media use, protecting personal information, and understanding digital footprint implications.

Security is strongest where awareness is highest.

Incident Reporting and Response Protocols

Clear Reporting Channels

Establishing accessible, confidential mechanisms for students and staff to report cyber incidents without fear.

Immediate Containment

Activating rapid response procedures to isolate affected systems and prevent further damage or data loss.

Recovery and Communication

Implementing systematic recovery plans while maintaining transparent communication with parents, authorities, and stakeholders.

The safest network is a well-informed community.

CHAPTER SEVEN

EMPOWERING TEACHERS AND ADMINISTRATORS

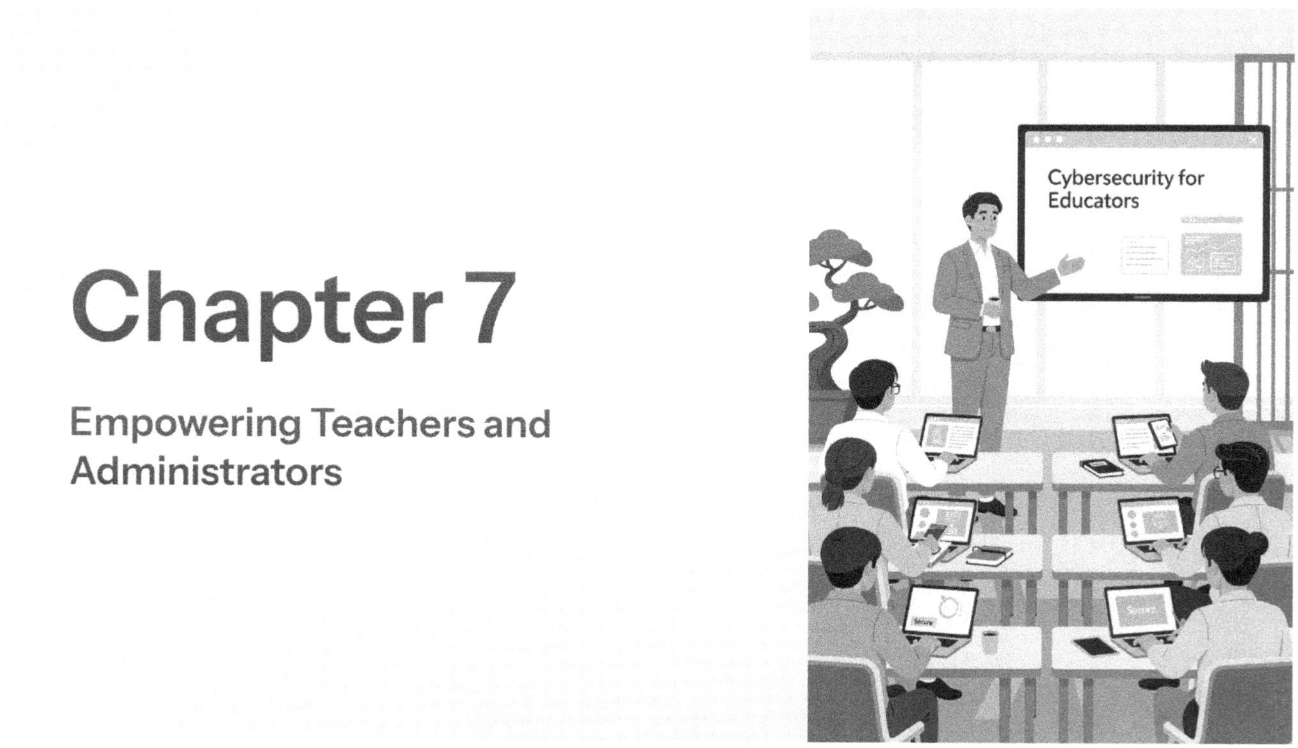

Online safety begins with personal responsibility.

Cybersecurity Training for Educators

Comprehensive Training Approach

- Tailored modules addressing common threats specific to educational settings
- Hands-on workshops with realistic scenarios and simulations
- Regular refresher courses to stay current with evolving threats
- Certification programmes recognizing cyber safety expertise

Building a culture of vigilance and responsibility where every educator understands their role in maintaining digital safety.

Cyber threats exploit ignorance more than intelligence.

Role of School Leadership

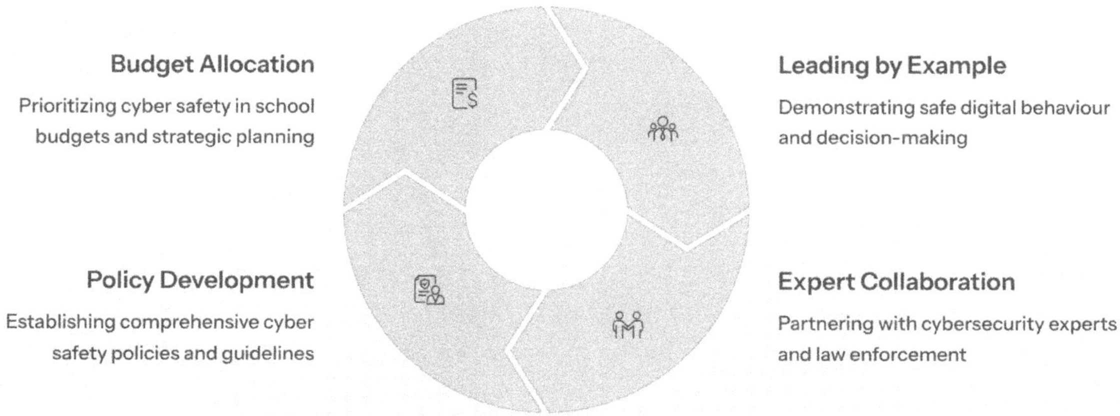

Protect your data as carefully as you protect your identity.

Supporting Teachers in Rural and Under-Resourced Areas

Mobile Training Units

Bringing cyber safety education directly to remote schools through mobile labs and traveling training teams equipped with necessary resources.

Online Resources

Providing accessible digital learning materials, video tutorials, and virtual support communities for self-paced professional development.

Partnership Networks

Collaborating with NGOs, government programmes, and corporate social responsibility initiatives to expand reach and impact.

Continuous Learning Incentives

Offering recognition, career advancement opportunities, and financial support for teachers pursuing cyber safety expertise.

Digital safety is a habit, not a one-time action.

CHAPTER EIGHT

PROTECTING STUDENTS ONLINE

Schools must teach cyber values along with cyber skills.

Age-Appropriate Digital Literacy Curriculum

1. Primary Grades (6-10 years)

Basic internet safety, recognizing trusted adults online, understanding privacy, and identifying inappropriate content.

2. Middle School (11-14 years)

Social media safety, digital footprints, cyberbullying prevention, and responsible online communication.

3. High School (15-18 years)

Advanced privacy protection, critical evaluation of online information, understanding digital consent, and protecting personal data.

Technology empowers, but safety sustains.

Parental Involvement and Education

Empowering Parents as Digital Guardians

Conducting regular workshops to improve parents' understanding of digital platforms, risks, and safety strategies their children encounter daily.

Providing practical tools and guidance for monitoring age-appropriate online activity while respecting children's growing autonomy and privacy needs.

Encouraging open, non-judgmental communication about online experiences, creating safe spaces for children to discuss concerns without fear of device restrictions.

Technology empowers, but safety sustains.

Mental Health Support and Safe Spaces

Counselling Services

Providing accessible psychological support for victims of cyberbullying, online harassment, and digital stress through trained counsellors.

Peer Support Groups

Creating student-led awareness clubs and support networks where learners can share experiences and strategies in safe environments.

Digital Wellness

Promoting balanced screen time, encouraging offline activities, and teaching mindfulness techniques to manage digital consumption.

A secure digital culture starts with ethical use.

Fostering Open Dialogue on Online Safety

Building trust and creating a safe space for conversation is crucial. Encourage children to share their online experiences, both positive and challenging, without fear of judgment. This open dialogue empowers them to navigate the digital world responsibly and seek help when needed.

Regular, honest conversations strengthen your child's online resilience and deepen your connection. Start today!

Cyber security is not fear-driven; it is wisdom-driven.

CHAPTER NINE

Technology Solutions for School Cyber Safety

Every user is a gatekeeper of digital safety.

Cybersecurity Tools for Schools

Endpoint Protection

Enterprise-grade antivirus and anti-malware software protecting all devices accessing school networks and systems.

Content Filtering

Age-appropriate content filtering systems and parental control solutions preventing access to harmful websites and materials.

Secure LMS

Protected learning management systems with built-in security features, encrypted communications, and secure data storage.

Online spaces need the same rules as physical spaces.

Monitoring and Analytics

01

Real-Time Threat Detection

Advanced monitoring systems providing instant alerts for suspicious activities, unauthorized access attempts, and potential security breaches.

02

Behaviour Analytics

User behaviour analytics identifying unusual patterns that may indicate compromised accounts or insider threats requiring investigation.

03

Automated Backups

Regular automated data backups with disaster recovery plans ensuring business continuity even after significant cyber incidents.

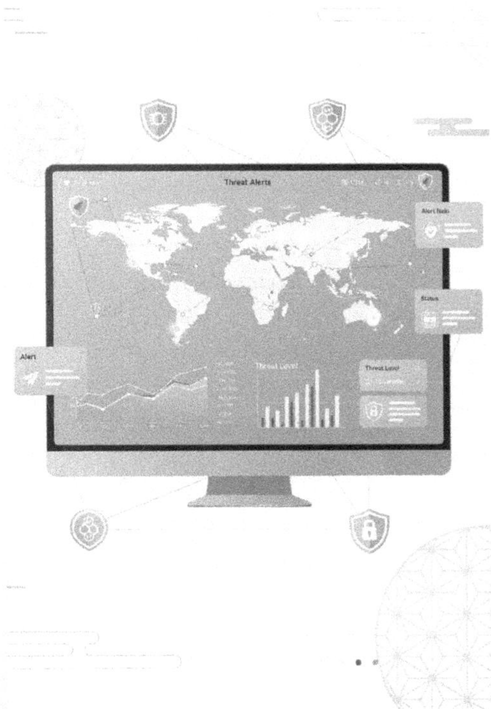

Cyber hygiene is as important as personal hygiene.

Collaboration with Cybersecurity Firms

Expert Partnership Benefits

- Access to specialized knowledge and 24/7 incident response teams
- Regular vulnerability assessments and penetration testing services
- Threat intelligence sharing and early warning systems
- Staff training and awareness programme support
- Cyber insurance options tailored for educational institutions

The weakest link in security is often human behaviour.

CHAPTER TEN

Case Studies and Success Stories

Digital safety is not a choice—it is a duty.

Pune and Thiruvallur School Cyber Safety Programs

40+	12K+	90%
Schools Trained	**Beneficiaries**	**Satisfaction Rate**
Educational institutions implementing comprehensive cyber safety programmes	Students, teachers, and parents reached through tailored modules	Participants reporting improved confidence in digital safety

These programmes demonstrated significant improvement in cyber awareness among students and teachers, with sustained behaviour changes months after training. Community outreach efforts successfully expanded the digital safety culture beyond school boundaries to families and neighbourhoods.

Technology thrives best in safe hands.

Government of India's Cyber Safety Handbook for Students

A comprehensive, widely distributed resource developed by the Ministry of Electronics and Information Technology, explaining cyber threats and safeguards in accessible language.

Key Features:

- Targeted at adolescents aged 13+ with age-appropriate content
- Practical tips for recognizing and responding to threats
- Emergency helpline information and reporting procedures
- Available in multiple Indian languages for nationwide reach
- Regular updates reflecting emerging digital risks

Cyber awareness is the shield of the digital age.

International Examples: Finland's Cyber Safety Curriculum

Finland's education system offers valuable lessons in comprehensive digital citizenship education.

Early Integration

Cyber safety concepts introduced from early grades, evolving in complexity as students progress through the education system.

Critical Thinking Focus

Emphasis on developing analytical skills to evaluate online information, identify manipulation, and make informed digital decisions.

Digital Citizenship

Holistic approach teaching rights, responsibilities, and ethical behaviour in digital spaces as core competencies.

A secure digital space enables fearless learning.

Empowering the Next Generation: Cyber Safety Achievers

Witness the triumph of young minds! These bright Indian students proudly display their certificates, marking the successful completion of their comprehensive cyber safety training. This achievement signifies not just knowledge gained, but a vital step towards responsible and secure digital citizenship.

Equipped with critical skills, they are now ready to navigate the online world with confidence, understanding the importance of privacy, identifying threats, and fostering a safe digital environment for themselves and their communities. Their dedication lights the way for a more secure digital future.

Safety is the foundation of digital innovation.

CHAPTER ELEVEN

Challenges and the Road Ahead

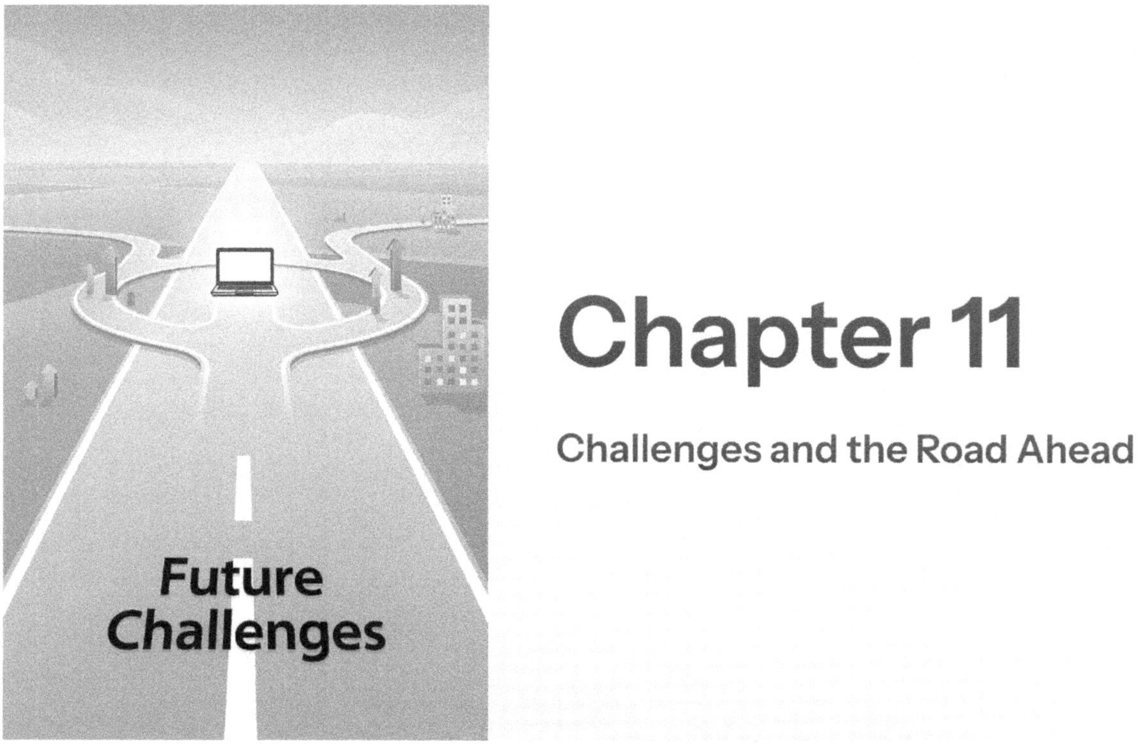

Cyber safety is the bridge between technology and trust.

Persistent Challenges

Access Inequality

Persistent disparities in technology access and quality training between urban and rural areas, affluent and economically disadvantaged schools.

Evolving Threat Landscape

Cyber threats advancing faster than awareness programmes, with new attack vectors and social engineering techniques constantly emerging.

Innovation vs. Safety Balance

The ongoing challenge of embracing digital innovation and new technologies while maintaining robust safety and privacy protections.

Secure practices today build trust for tomorrow.

Addressing Gender and Socioeconomic Gaps

Gender-Inclusive Approaches

Ensuring girls and young women have equal access to digital technologies and cyber safety education, addressing specific vulnerabilities they face online.

Creating safe spaces for female students to learn about technology without facing stereotypes or harassment.

Reaching Marginalized Groups

Developing tailored programmes for diverse linguistic, cultural, and socioeconomic contexts across India's varied landscape.

Addressing barriers like language, literacy levels, and cultural sensitivities in cyber safety education.

Online safety is the responsibility we owe future generations.

Strengthening Policy and Enforcement

Legislative Updates

Updating laws to comprehensively cover emerging cyber threats like deepfakes, AI-generated content, and sophisticated social engineering.

Inter-Agency Coordination

Enhancing collaboration between schools, local police, state cyber cells, and national agencies for effective prevention and response.

Accountability Mechanisms

Establishing clear accountability for cybersecurity lapses while supporting schools with resources rather than punitive measures.

Awareness transforms users into protectors.

Future Trends in School Cyber Safety

1

AI-Powered Protection

Artificial intelligence and machine learning systems providing adaptive threat detection, personalized safety recommendations, and automated incident response.

2

Digital Ethics Education

Growing emphasis on teaching ethical decision-making in digital spaces, addressing issues like AI bias, data privacy, and digital manipulation.

3

Peer-Led Initiatives

Expanding student-led cyber ambassador programs, leveraging peer influence for more effective safety message dissemination.

Cyber security is a culture, not a checklist.

CHAPTER TWELVE

CALL TO ACTION- BUILDING A CYBER SAFE SCHOOL ECOSYSTEM

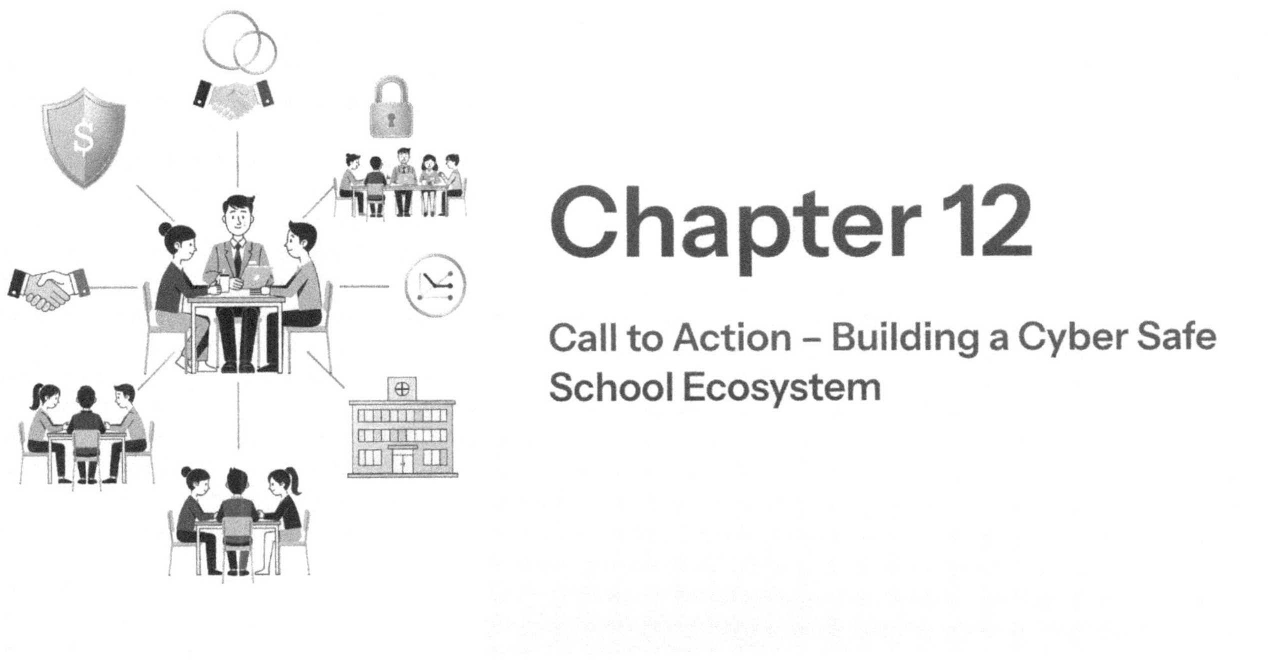

Responsible users create resilient systems.

For School Leaders

Strategic Investment

Prioritize cybersecurity infrastructure, training, and ongoing maintenance in institutional budgets and strategic planning documents.

Cultural Transformation

Foster an organizational culture valuing openness, continuous learning, and proactive safety rather than reactive crisis management.

Stakeholder Engagement

Actively involve parents, students, and community partners in developing and implementing comprehensive cyber safety policies.

Digital safety empowers confidence, not limitation.

For Educators

Professional Development

Commit to staying updated on evolving cyber threats, emerging technologies, and best practices through continuous professional learning.

Student Empowerment

Equip learners with knowledge, critical thinking skills, and confidence to navigate digital spaces safely and responsibly.

Role Modeling

Demonstrate safe digital practices in your own online presence and professional use of technology.

Every login is an opportunity to stay safe.

For Parents and Guardians

1 **Active Digital Parenting**

Engage meaningfully in children's digital lives through open conversations, shared online experiences, and age-appropriate monitoring.

2 **Home Safety Practices**

Promote balanced, safe technology use at home with clear guidelines, device-free times, and positive digital role modeling.

3 **Partnership with Schools**

Actively participate in school cyber safety initiatives, workshops, and maintain regular communication with educators.

Online safety is about foresight, not fear.

For Policymakers and Partners

Scalable Programme Support

Provide sustained funding, resources, and policy support for cyber safety programmes that can reach schools across diverse contexts nationwide.

Public-Private Partnerships

Encourage innovative collaborations between government, educational institutions, technology companies, and civil society for comprehensive solutions.

Evidence-Based Policy

Support research, data collection, and evaluation to inform effective policies and continuously improve cyber safety interventions.

Secure behaviour creates secure environments.

Together Towards a Safer Digital Future for Our Schools

Here to Stay

Digital education is permanent—let's protect it with vigilance and knowledge

Empower Everyone

Every child and educator deserves to navigate cyberspace safely and confidently

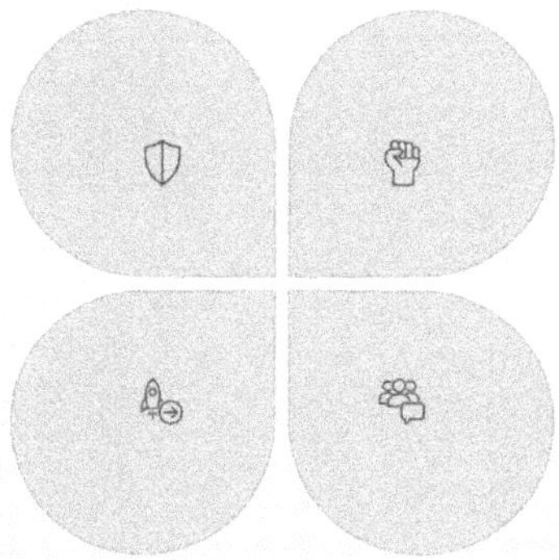

Bright Tomorrow

Together, we can create a secure digital future for the next generation

Join the Movement

Transform schools into cyber safe havens through collective action

The journey to comprehensive cyber safety requires commitment from all stakeholders. Start today—every step towards digital safety is a step towards protecting our children's future.

Technology without safety is risk without reward.

CHAPTER THIRTEEN

CYBER SECURITY TIPS

Cyber Security Tips for Students, Teachers & Parents

In today's interconnected digital world, cybersecurity is no longer optional —it's essential. This guide empowers students, teachers, and parents with practical strategies to navigate online spaces safely and confidently.

A secure future begins with safe digital choices today.

CHAPTER 1

Why Cybersecurity Matters for Everyone

The digital landscape has transformed how we learn, teach, and communicate. Understanding cybersecurity risks and protective measures is now a fundamental life skill for every member of our educational community.

Schools are the first line of cyber defence for children.

The Digital World is Our Classroom and Playground

Students Online

Spending countless hours engaging with educational platforms, social media, and entertainment whilst navigating complex digital environments daily.

Teachers' Digital Responsibility

Managing sensitive student data, operating virtual classrooms, and safeguarding confidential academic information across multiple platforms.

Parents Balancing Act

Juggling the challenge of protecting family privacy whilst guiding children towards developing safe, responsible online habits and digital literacy.

Awareness turns vulnerability into strength.

17% of Teachers Report Cybersecurity Breaches Linked to Students

Unsafe online behaviour can lead to serious real-world consequences affecting entire school communities. The statistics paint a concerning picture of current digital vulnerabilities.

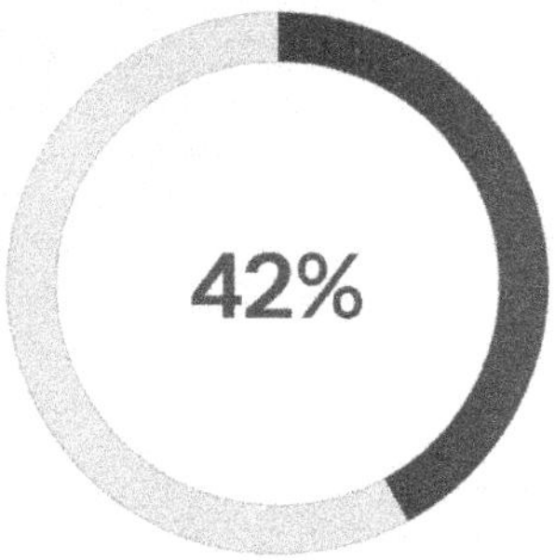

Serious Incidents

Teachers aware of significant online safety incidents involving their students

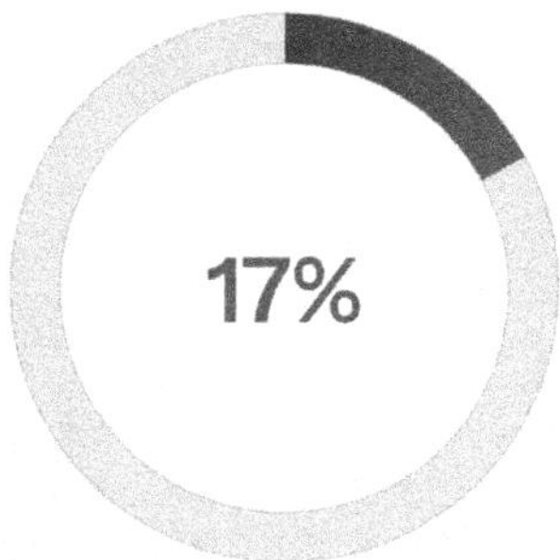

Security Breaches

Schools experiencing cybersecurity breaches directly linked to student actions

Cybersecurity safeguards not just systems, but people.

One Click Can Cost Everything

A single moment of inattention or poor judgement can expose personal information, compromise accounts, and create lasting digital consequences. Vigilance and awareness are your strongest defences.

Protect your data; it tells your story.

CHAPTER 2

Cyber Threats Students Face Daily

Understanding the specific risks lurking in digital spaces is the first step towards building robust defences. Students encounter multiple threat vectors every single day online.

Online safety is the new literacy.

Phishing & Smishing: The Scams You Must Spot

Phishing Attacks

Fraudulent emails or deceptive websites designed to trick you into revealing personal information, passwords, or financial details through convincing impersonation.

Smishing Threats

Similar scams delivered via text messages—less known but rapidly rising. These SMS-based attacks exploit trust in mobile communication channels.

Alarming Gap in Awareness

36% of parents remain completely unaware of smishing risks, leaving families vulnerable to this growing threat vector that targets mobile devices.

Digital responsibility defines digital maturity.

Oversharing & Privacy Risks on Social Media

52%

Teachers Witnessing Oversharing

Educators observing students routinely sharing excessive personal information on social platforms

What Students Often Share Unsafely:

- Real-time location data and check-ins
- Daily schedules and routines
- School names and specific locations
- Family information and home addresses
- Photos revealing identifying details

Privacy settings are frequently ignored, misunderstood, or incorrectly configured, leaving digital footprints that can be exploited by malicious actors or impact future opportunities.

Safe technology use reflects strong values.

Cyberbullying and Digital Reputation

01

Unsafe Posts Create Vulnerabilities

Inappropriate content can trigger bullying, harassment, or unwanted attention from peers and strangers alike.

02

Think Before Posting

Students must understand that digital content can have permanent consequences affecting relationships, opportunities, and mental wellbeing.

03

Guidance is Essential

Teachers and parents play crucial roles in helping young people develop digital wisdom and resilience against online threats.

Security is not about restriction; it is about protection.

CHAPTER 3

Strong Passwords & Authentication

Your passwords are the keys to your digital kingdom. Creating and maintaining strong authentication practices forms the foundation of personal cybersecurity.

A moment of awareness can prevent years of damage.

Passwords: Your First Line of Defence

Length & Complexity

Use passwords with at least 12 characters combining uppercase, lowercase, numbers, and special symbols

Never Share

Keep passwords completely private—even trusted friends shouldn't know your credentials

Use Passphrases

Create memorable combinations like "BlueFish!2026" that are both strong and easier to remember

Pro Tip: Avoid using personal information like birthdates, pet names, or common words. Each account should have a unique password to prevent cascading breaches.

Trust online should be built slowly and verified always.

Multi-Factor Authentication (MFA)

Adding a Critical Security Layer

MFA requires a second verification step beyond your password—typically a code sent to your phone, biometric scan, or authentication app confirmation.

8%

Current Parent Understanding

Only a small fraction of parents fully comprehend MFA today

Essential Protection For:

- Email accounts and cloud storage
- School learning management portals
- Banking and financial applications
- Social media platforms

Cyber safety protects children before threats reach them.

Double Up Your Security with MFA

Even if someone discovers your password, multi-factor authentication ensures they cannot access your accounts without the second verification factor. Enable it everywhere possible.

Prevention is always cheaper than recovery.

CHAPTER 4

Safe Online Habits for Students

Developing consistent, secure online behaviours transforms cybersecurity from a burden into second nature. These practical habits protect you daily.

Smart users make safe systems.

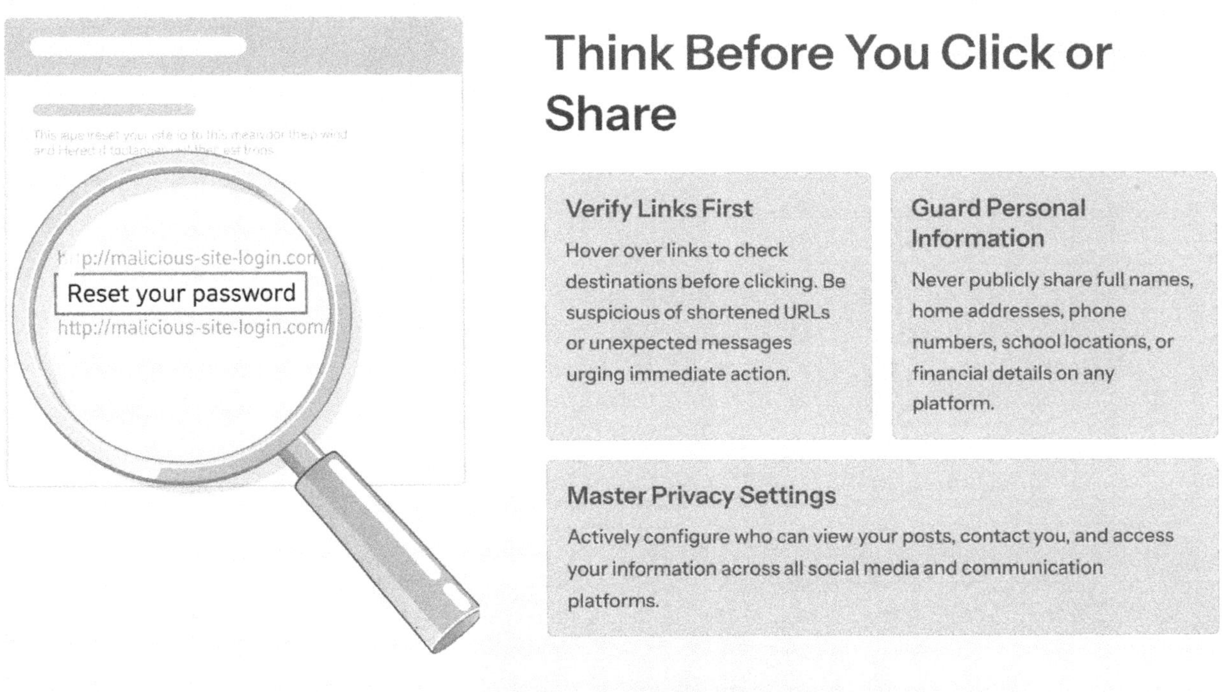

Digital safety is a shared commitment.

Regular Backups & Software Updates

1 Backup Schoolwork

Save important files to cloud storage or external drives regularly to prevent data loss from device failures or ransomware attacks

2 Update Antivirus

Keep security software current and run regular system scans to detect threats before they cause damage

3 Patch Systems

Install operating system and application updates promptly —they fix known security vulnerabilities that hackers exploit

Set reminders to back up critical files weekly. Enable automatic updates where possible to ensure you're always protected against the latest threats.

Knowledge is the strongest defence against cybercrime.

CHAPTER 5

Teachers' Role in Cybersecurity

Educators stand at the frontline of digital safety, responsible for both protecting sensitive data and cultivating cybersecurity awareness in the next generation.

Cybersecurity protects learning, leadership, and lives.

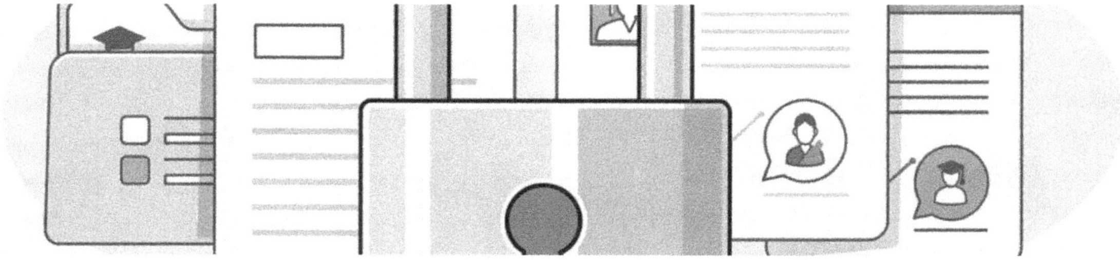

Protecting Student Privacy is a Legal & Ethical Duty

1

Understand Legal Requirements

Familiarise yourself with FERPA (Family Educational Rights and Privacy Act) and student data privacy rights that govern information handling.

2

Use Secure Platforms

Communicate through verified, encrypted channels for grading, parent communication, and sharing sensitive student information.

3

Report Suspicious Activity

Immediately alert IT departments or school administration about unusual access attempts, data breaches, or potential security threats.

Responsible use is the foundation of digital safety.

Cybersecurity Training & Curriculum Gaps

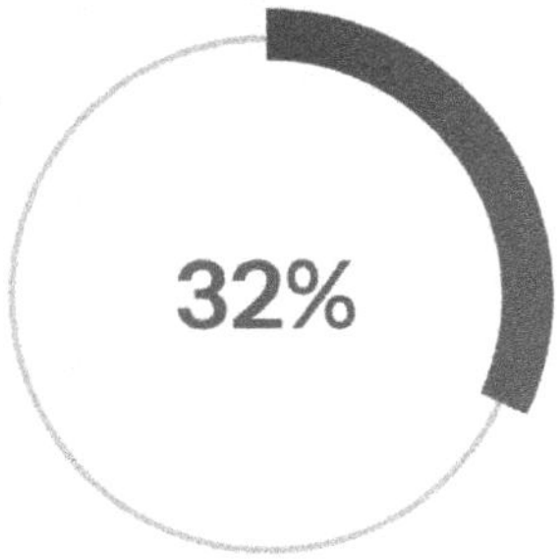

Trained Teachers

Educators receiving formal training on online safety protocols

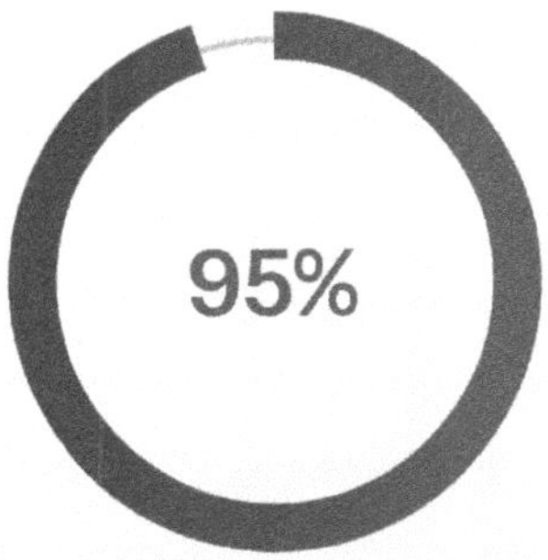

Support Mandatory Education

Teachers believing cybersecurity should be required curriculum

The Critical Need for Resources

Teachers require comprehensive training materials, lesson plans, and ongoing professional development to confidently teach digital safety concepts.

Without proper preparation, educators struggle to address evolving cyber threats and answer student questions effectively.

The weakest link in security is often human behaviour.

CHAPTER 6

Parents as Cybersecurity Guides

Parents serve as primary influences in shaping children's digital habits and values. Your guidance creates the foundation for lifelong cybersecurity awareness.

Cyber hygiene is as important as personal hygiene.

Open Communication Builds Trust & Awareness

Regular Discussions

Talk frequently about online experiences, both positive and concerning. Create a judgement-free space for sharing digital encounters and asking questions.

Encourage Reporting

Empower children to immediately report suspicious messages, uncomfortable interactions, cyberbullying, or anything that feels wrong without fear of punishment.

Establish Clear Boundaries

Set reasonable, age-appropriate limits on screen time, device usage times, and which platforms or apps are permitted with explanations for your decisions.

Online spaces need the same rules as physical spaces.

Tools Parents Can Use

Antivirus & Parental Controls

Install reputable security software like Net Nanny that filters content, monitors activity, and protects against malware across all family devices.

Password Management

Use password managers or child-friendly generators like DinoPass to create and store strong, unique passwords safely without memorisation stress.

Privacy Configuration

Regularly review and adjust privacy settings on social media platforms, school apps, and any services your children use to limit data exposure.

Every user is a gatekeeper of digital safety.

Cyber Safety Starts at Home

The habits, values, and awareness you instil today will protect your children throughout their digital lives. Make cybersecurity a family priority and conversation topic.

Cybersecurity is not fear-driven; it is wisdom-driven.

CHAPTER 7

Building a Safer Digital Future Together

Creating secure digital environments requires collective effort, shared responsibility, and ongoing commitment from every member of our educational ecosystem.

A secure digital culture starts with ethical use.

Cybersecurity is Everyone's Responsibility

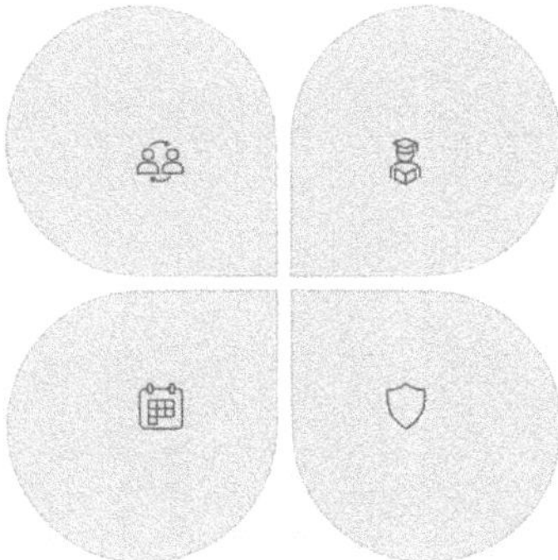

Collaborate & Share Knowledge

Students, teachers, and parents must work together, communicate openly, and stay informed about evolving threats

Empower Through Education

Equip yourself with knowledge, tools, and resources to confidently navigate digital spaces safely

Start Today

Make cybersecurity a daily habit, not an afterthought—your digital safety begins right now

Create Secure Environments

Together we build protective spaces where learning and growth happen without compromise

Take Action Now: Review your passwords, enable MFA on critical accounts, discuss online safety with your family, and commit to staying vigilant. Small steps today create significant protection tomorrow.

Awareness today prevents regret tomorrow.

CHAPTER FOURTEEN

Cyber Safety FAQs with Simple Answers

For Students

1. What does it mean to be secure online?
Cyber safety involves protecting yourself while using digital devices, apps, mobile phones, and the internet.

2. Why do students need to be secure online?
It keeps you safe from online threats, including bullying, scams, misinformation, and misuse of your personal information.

3. What should I do if I get a link or message that seems fishy?
Don't click on it. Tell your parents or instructors right away.

4. How can I make a password that is hard to guess?
Mix letters, numbers, and symbols together. Do not give out your name or date of birth.

5. Is it safe to reveal private information on the internet?
No. Don't ever give out your address, phone number, school name, or passwords.

6. What is cyberbullying?
When someone uses the internet to injure, scare, or humiliate someone else, that's cyberbullying.

7. What should I do if someone is bullying me online?
Keep proof, block the person, and tell a trusted adult.

8. Is it safe to trust anyone you meet online?
No. People on the internet could not be who they say they are.

9. Why should I ponder before I post on social media?
Once something is posted, it can stay online forever and change your life.

10. What is a digital footprint?
It's the record of everything you do on the internet.

11. Is it always safe to download games or apps for free?
No. Some apps contain viruses or steal your information.

12. Why shouldn't I tell my pals my passwords?
Passwords keep your accounts and personal information safe.

13. What is phishing?
Scammers use phishing to trick you into giving them your personal information.

14. How can you tell whether a website is fake?
Look for spelling mistakes, weird links, and sources you don't know.

15. Is it safe and right to use AI or internet technologies for schoolwork?
Don't use them to copy answers; use them to help you learn.

For Parents

16. What are some of the most common dangers kids face on the internet today?
Cyberbullying, being addicted to screens, hazardous content, and online frauds.

17. How much time should kids spend in front of screens?
It depends on their age, but it's important to find a balance between time spent outside and time with family.

18. How can parents keep an eye on what their kids do online without compromising their privacy?
Talk to each other honestly and make sure everyone knows the rules.

19. What are parental controls, and how do they work?
They keep kids away from bad content and limit how much time they spend on screens.

20. How can parents communicate to their kids about staying safe online?
Use real-life examples and plain language.

21. What are some symptoms that a child might be being bullied online?
Changes in mood, fear of devices, or retreat.

22. Are social networking sites safe for kids?
For safety concerns, most platforms impose age limits.

23. What can parents do to keep their kids' personal information safe online?
Don't share too much and teach your kids about privacy.

24. What should parents do if their child shares private information without meaning to?
Act fast, change your passwords, and tell someone about the problem.

25. How can parents help their kids use AI tools in a responsible way?
Talk about how to use things in a moral way and how to utilise them to learn.

26. How do parents help their kids learn digital discipline?
Parents need to show their kids how to use technology safely and in a balanced way.

27. How can parents keep up with new online threats?
Follow school announcements and news from sources you trust.

28. What can be done legally in the case of significant cyber incidents?
People can report cybercrime to the police.

29. How can parents show their kids how to be safe online?
By utilising strong passwords and being polite while talking to people online.

30. Why is it necessary to be able to talk to each other openly when it comes to cyber safety?
Kids will tell you about problems without being scared.

For Teachers

31. Why is it vital for schools to teach kids about cyber safety?
Students need to understand how to behave safely online as soon as possible.

32. How can schools include online safety in their lessons?
Through teachings in value education, ICT, and life skills.

33. What are the most common cyber threats that schools face?
Data breaches, device misuse, and online bullying.

34. How can teachers tell if pupils are being bullied online?
Look for changes in behaviour and concerns from peers.

35. What should schools do to keep student data safe?
Use safe systems and limit who can see the data.

36. How can teachers encourage kids to act ethically online?
By teaching people how to be responsible, respectful, and honest online.

37. What part do instructors play in teaching kids how to be good digital citizens?
Teachers help kids learn to behave safely and respectfully online.

38. What can schools do to make the internet a safe place?
Through rules, training, and awareness-raising programs.

39. What rules should schools have to keep kids safe online?
Policies for data protection, acceptable use, and cyberbullying.

40. How can AI tools be used in schools without putting students at risk?
With rules, monitoring, and lessons in ethics.

41. What should schools do if there is a cyber safety incident?
Act swiftly, help the affected students, and notify their parents.

42. Why is it important for staff to learn about cyber safety?
To help their students, teachers need to know about hazards.

43. How can schools get parents involved in programs to keep kids safe online?
Through meetings, bulletins, and workshops.

44. Why are privacy and consent important in schools?
It is important to keep students' personal information safe.

45. How can digital learning deal with false information?
Teach people how to check facts and think critically.

Based on general knowledge and awareness

46. What's the difference between cyber safety and cyber security?
Cyber safety is about acting safely, whereas cyber security is about keeping systems safe.

47. How does cyber safety help keep your mind healthy?
It reduces tension, fear, and online bullying.

48. What makes cyber safety everyone's job?
Digital safety is affected by what everyone does.

49. How often should the guidelines for being safe online be checked?
At least once a year.

50. What can students, parents, and teachers do together to make the internet safer?
By talking to one another, working together, and following the same safety regulations.

About The Author

Dr. Dheeraj Mehrotra is a distinguished educational leader with over three decades of experience, he has been a driving force in transforming education through innovation and excellence. A recipient of the **President of India's National Teacher Award (2006)**, Dr. Mehrotra is a certified expert in **Six Sigma, NLP, and TQM**, specializing in **academic audits, SQAA**, and implementing **Kaizen and 5S practices** in schools.

An accomplished author, he has published over **200 books** on topics ranging from computer science and AI to school management and quality circles. His contribution includes developing **150+ free educational mobile apps**, earning him recognition in the **Limca Book of Records** and **India Book of Records**.

http://www.authordheerajmehrotra.com

Books By The Same Author

www.ingramcontent.com/pod-product-compliance
Lightning Source LLC
LaVergne TN
LVHW071410210926
848486LV00004B/240
9798902692188